IN SOLITUDE

IN SOLITUDE

A much needed 'PEACE OF MIND' is found in solitude.

Copyright © Ed Breeding November 5, 2023

IN SOLITUDE
-PREFACE-

You may ask, "What is the importance of solitude?", and the answer to that question is legion. It has been said that ninety-five percent of our human species are takers, and only five percent of us are givers. In anyone's calculation, that is very extreme, and...questionable, but...perhaps we should ask our individual self, am I a taker or a giver?

If we study the great achievers and givers throughout history, whether they were inventors, scientists, philosophers, artists, authors, teachers and many others who have contributed greatly to the benefit of mankind, we will learn that most all of them, created their contributions IN SOLITUDE.

Perhaps you are an author or a painter. Can you write a book or create a painting in the midst of other people? No... I think not. You must have solitude to think, gather your ideas and then...create. And that does not diminish the joy and importance of spending quality time with other people. It's about priority, balance and discipline in our lives at certain times. But if you know of anyone that you admire and respect that is a creator, you will, no doubt, learn that what they created, which you greatly enjoyed and appreciated, it had been created in solitude, where there were no interruptions or disturbances.

IN SOLITUDE is where we go to pray and meditate, and...to be able to connect and commune with the Spirit world. Perhaps we have all heard of 'the still small voice.' And that 'voice' cannot be heard in the midst of disruptions, noise and confusion. It has been said that prayer is us talking to Great Spirit/Creator/God, and Instinct/Intuition is Great Spirit/Creator/God talking to us, and again, that must take place in solitude. To be a truly Spiritual person, which entails listening to, understanding, hearing and connecting with the Spiritual realm, that must take place in solitude, in order to achieve the greatest benefit.

One of mankind's greatest fears is the "unknown." And many people are afraid of being alone; they feel safer around others, but whenever they experience the great benefits, they receive from being in solitude, they will soon seek it at every opportunity, and that need not dismiss quality time spent with family and friends.

Perhaps one of the greatest gifts we can receive from being in solitude is when we are able to see, feel, and truly appreciate some of the smaller things around us, whether it's a small flower by the sidewalk, or the bird in a tree, but by being in a crowd or with a group of other people, we overlook or totally miss those things that great thinkers, and creators see, feel, appreciate, love, and incorporate into their wonderful creations which we enjoy and appreciate. Being in solitude does not mean that we should not be around and spend time with other people, and it does not mean being lonely; basically, in solitude means where great and important lessons are learned, and inspiration and creations are created. Loneliness and solitude seem very similar on the outside, but the only characteristic both have in common is the state of physical solitude.

IN SOLITUDE   ED BREEDING

Chapter 1

We are born into a family, and soon we are in social settings with other people. Through those human experiences we quickly learn about what is important, good, bad, wanted and unwanted in our life. But we are each born with an indwelling spirit which is connected to the Great Spirit of all. And in our earliest years of physical life, after coming from the Spiritual realm, we are guided by our indwelling spirit, and that is when we first develop our own, unique personality. That personality will be affected by others around us, but inside ourselves, we will always be a unique and different individual from everyone else. And from those earliest and formative years, it is when we are able to be alone…in solitude; that is when we get in tune with who we really are and with our "Higher Self." An example of this may be of a child at three or four years of age, and the mother hears her young daughter humming a tune that has never been heard before. And when the mother realizes that her child has a gift for writing and singing songs, that can be the beginning of an iconic singer's later life, whose great musical gift is able to enrich many of our own lives.

If we can take the time to think back on some of our earliest childhood memories, we may be able to recall some instances when we were alone, and perhaps, playing in a nearby field or forest, or beside a stream, and we became impressed by what we were seeing and experiencing, and that imprint on our early life could be very important and effective in our life-journey ahead.

On the highway of life, at random and various times, we are all takers and givers. But, what makes all the difference is in how much we take versus how much we give back or give to others. It is in solitude, with our God-given gift, where we are able to create something different from everyone else, which is appreciated, needed and wanted by others. And many people may cop out and say, "Oh, I'm not talented or gifted," but that isn't true. Gifts come in many different and various shapes, sizes, colors and energies. The important lesson is to learn what your gift is, and then how best to share it with the world, and it is in solitude, alone with your 'Higher Self,' where you will discover your gift in life. And…your gift may be: being kind and loving to a stranger, a great ditch digger, sharing what you have with the needy, being a great listener and giving feedback, et cetera. Where the Holy Bible speaks about "the Kingdom of God is within us," that 'Kingdom' is our Spirit-our Higher Self.

Some may think that it is very lonely being alone in nature, but those that are awakened to their Sacred Earth Mother's gifts, in solitude, nature is where some of the greatest and unforgettable experiences in life can take place. For example, when sitting beneath a large tree in the forest and getting into a meditative state, it is possible…if you have learned how to listen, to hear some of the great wisdom that the tree has gained from its many years of growth in the splendor of the 'talking forest.' The limbs of trees reach out and gather universal messages, and those messages are absorbed in the leaves/needles of the tree. Eventually the leaves and needles detach from the 'source' and fall to the ground, where they decay for a season and are then reborn into the essence of the source, the tree.

The tree is a metaphor for our Creator/God, and the leaves/needles represent the birth-life-death-rebirth of the human being. And so....as this all takes place in solitude, what better example can we be given for the power and importance of solitude, than the tree in the forest?

Many of us have heard the statement: Oh, he/she is a tree hugger! And typically, when that statement has been made, it has been said in a sarcastic or ridiculing way, in an attempt to belittle someone that loves to spend time in the forest with trees, or in nature in general. But sadly for the ridiculing person, they have no idea about the amount of positive energy that can be stored in a tree, and whenever we hug, touch, sit beneath or merely caress the tree, or its leaves and needles, with the right attitude and intention, we are able to absorb some of that energy, which in turn...it has the potential to heal us from an emotional, mental or physical infirmity. But for this to happen, it is first necessary that we are in a prayerful, meditative state of mind in order to allow this process to happen, and...again, it is in solitude and being alone in nature where miracles can happen. And being alone in solitude, means just that! Alone with our Higher Self, excluding another person or pet. And you may ask? Why so? Because, having another person or pet with you can be a distraction, whereby you may miss the messages from nature and the universe, which you could receive, by being alone...IN SOLITUDE.

****

Different people have different ways to meditate, but for this writer, the essence of meditating for me is to, first and foremost, get in solitude, and that entails detaching from all sounds, people and things around me, especially electronic devices, and be still in solitude. If your mind is spinning, cut it off and imagine via your third eye a blank screen, focusing on it, and allow whatever images may choose to appear on that blank screen, but do not attach or over think with the mind. The better we can still the over-active mind, the better the meditation process. And calling on my Spirit Guides of Love and Light have always been great helpers for me, but I never forget to thank them for guiding me in love and light. Some of our Spirit Guides could possibly be a deceased loved one. During a 'Past Lives Regression' in the year 2000, the practitioner said that I had a very powerful Native American wanting to be one of my 'guides,' and of course, I accepted and needed him. Since that time, I have been very fortunate, for most all of my Traditional Indigenous documentaries to be constantly shown across the country via FNX (First Nations Experience) TV on PBS Affiliate station, into 82 million households, thanks in part to my good Apache friend, Geronimo Vela, who initiated the process, and my Spirit Guides of Love and Light.

****

The world around us can oftentimes be a very 'cold' place, and in groups of people there is often confusion, division and a multitude of distractions. Many people love to be in crowds of other people, feeling that they are not alone, and that is fine, but the question arises, what are you achieving, what are you creating, and does that improve or enhance your Sacred Mission on Planet Earth? In solitude, where our most important creations take place, the creating process is unending.

In today's world, wherever large crowds of people are gathered, we sometimes see violent outbreaks, and those crowds can also be targets for terrorists, and others that want to do harm or kill people, but that does not occur in solitude. If we want to learn why certain people seek to do harm and kill other people, we may learn that there is something inside themselves that they hate, dislike, or seek to destroy, and instead of dealing with their own negative issue in a healthful way, they project that negativity outward, onto others. Perhaps one of the best examples of this is with World dictators, or…would be dictators. They have a 'demon' inside themselves, and refusing to deal with it constructively, they project it outwards, onto others. This may be how many wars are started.

IN SOLITUDE   ED BREEDING

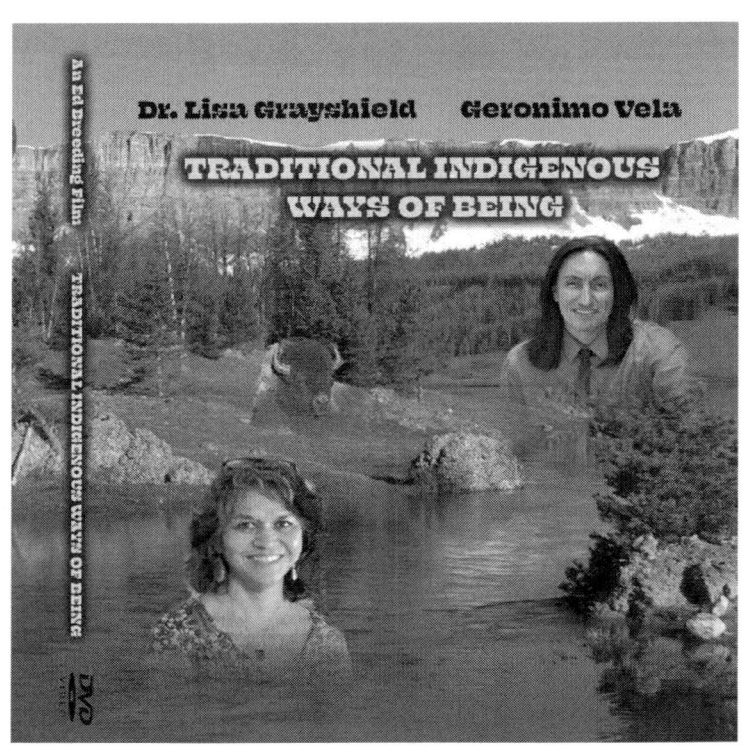

IN SOLITUDE ED BREEDING

IN SOLITUDE   ED BREEDING

Chapter 2

As children, we were often asked, "What are you going to be when you grow up?"

For many of us in the world, perhaps that question lingered and returned to us during many times in our young and formative years. While some youth have said they wanted to be doctors, lawyers, teachers, football players, actors, etc... maybe there have been some in their youth that just wanted to grow up and be a good and happy person. And what is your definition of a good person? And when we say that all we want in life is just to be happy, as we grow older, have we learned that what oftentimes makes us happy, is what makes us the saddest when we lose that person or thing? Peace, found in solitude, supersedes happiness!

Although many of us may not think of it this way, having and maintaining a peace of mind, in the long run, far outreaches being temporarily happy. And did not Jesus the Christ speak of leaving "Peace" with us? Peace of mind can be much richer than silver or gold, because it can sustain us when things in our lives don't go as we had hope they would, but with peace of mind, we survive and deal with the sad or bad issues in a mature and balanced way. And we may wish to consider that in order to have and maintain a peace of mind, spending time in solitude with our Higher Self, and getting our goals and priorities straight can best assure us of a continual peace of mind. And…didn't Jesus spend forty days and nights alone in the wilderness? We can only imagine what He may have accomplished there, being alone.

While in solitude, think of what is most important in life…for you. Is it security, family, job, sports, having a good time, or…do you wish to be a person that honors your Sacred Spiritual Contract, and does good deeds and contributes to the betterment of mankind? These are important issues for us all to consider, if…we want to have a peace of mind during our life-journey here on Planet Earth. And to achieve that goal, we may need to step out of our "comfort zone," which may consist of your immediate family, a small circle of friends and acquaintances, and open your mind and heart to things and those outside of your comfort zone.

****

After getting honorably discharged from the U.S. Air Force and living in Michigan, I had saved two thousand dollars while being in Germany. I asked an older brother's best friend, whom I highly respected, how I could best invest the money, and he suggest that I purchase land with it. He had forty acres of forested land in north central Michigan, and he helped me also find vacant land in that area where I purchased forty acres for $2,000.00, but…that was many years ago. The land was adjacent to the Manistee National Forest, and I spent many wonderful days there alone in solitude, and also with some family members and friends. As I had a managerial position at that time with La-Z-Boy Chair Company in Monroe, Michigan, driving up to my forest land on weekends was a great escape from the busy work schedule, and it was always a place and time in solitude to reflect and reenergize myself. During a summer, two-week vacation I decided to begin building a one-room cabin on my property, and build it on the border with the national forest. Prior to building the cabin, I had purchased a small, travel trailer about 12-foot-long, and while building the cabin I stayed in the trailer.

Some family members and friends enjoyed my 'getaway' as much as I did, and I gave them access to it whenever they liked, but often I was there alone in solitude, and from that time of being alone in a wilderness area and greatly enjoying the wildlife, such as deer and wild turkey, I began to delve into doing paintings of wildlife. And that was the beginning of my ultimate career of, not only becoming a painter, but painting led me to making independent documentary films and writing books. And to date, I have produced 21 documentary films and self-published 18 books on Amazon. But without that valuable time spent in solitude, where I was able to let my ideas germinate, perhaps I may never have accomplished what I believe has been my 'SACRED CONTRACT.' And my definition of a Sacred Contract is: before we are born and still in the Spirit realm, we, metaphorically speaking, sign a contract to use the gifts which we have been given to share with the betterment of mankind.

While I was Superintendent with La-Z-Boy Chair Company in Tennessee, some of my Department Heads and Foremen were having problems in dealing with the people under their supervision. And during a meeting I was having with them one day, I presented this idea for them to contemplate and consider: A mud puddle is small, shallow, smelly, but it is considered, WATER! A pond is larger than a mud puddle, but it has boundaries, not very deep, becomes stagnant, but is considered, WATER! And then…there is a fresh flowing stream, with new and fresh energy flowing into it, and it shares its freshness with all those which want to partake of it, and then in goes out and shares itself with the beyond... as WATER.

For my subordinates, my message for them was this: in life, as a metaphor, you can choose to be a mud puddle, a pond, or...a fresh flowing stream. The choice is yours. Like water, you will still be called a human, but the point is!: what kind of human do you want to be? If a person is unsure of who or what he/she wants to be, then going into solitude and spending time with your Higher Self is where the answer may be found.

While in my managerial position, an employee came to my office one morning and asked if he could speak with me, and of course, I said yes, but first, I asked if he had spoken to his supervisor, and his response was that he was not able to talk with his supervisor because the supervisor did not care about him or his situation.

And when I asked what he wished to talk about, he responded: "I told my supervisor that I had an emergency at home and needed to leave work immediately. He never asked what my emergency was or if he could help in any way, he just gave me permission to leave my job. And, well…I got in the parking lot, and I asked myself, what am I doing? I don't have an emergency at home, and I need to work in order to provide for my family!"

When I asked why he lied to his supervisor, he replied, "I was an adopted child, and I have lived in four different foster homes, but during all that, I have never felt truly loved, and I lied to my supervisor to see if he cared enough about me to at least ask what my emergency was, but…he didn't ask, and he didn't care about me."

That incident happened over thirty years ago in Tennessee, but I have never forgotten it.

And you may wonder, what did I do about my employee's situation, and first and foremost, I truthfully told him what a wonderful and valuable employee he was. I let him know that he was always on time for work, and that he was one of the greatest and most productive upholsterers we ever had in our factory, and that was true. I did not exaggerate for him. I also let him know that I would be having a serious talk with his supervisor, and all the other supervisors, about the importance of getting to know and caring about their employees.

Whether we are a supervisor over other people, or whatever our position in life may be, to be at peace with ourselves in life, it is very important to learn the very important lesson that we are a family of all humanity, and we must step out of our comfort zone when the situation calls for it, and realize that every single individual is just as important as our own little circle of family and friends, and…as a Spiritually awakened and evolved human being, it is our duty to show love and concern for them, when they are in need, and when it is in our power to do so, just as we show to those few in our "comfort zone." It is imperative to understand, that if we desire to evolve and grow as a Spiritual human being, it is necessary to expand the size of our comfort zone so large, whereby, we cannot see its boundaries.

When speaking of spirituality, it is important to understand the difference between religion and spirituality. Religions are organizations set up by man, and since every man is different from the next, so are many of the world's religions, but with spirituality, there is only one Great Spirit, Creator, God, and in spirituality, we recognize that we are a part of and connected to the Source/God. A Spiritually awakened person is guided by their Higher Self, whereas a religious person is usually guided by the dictates of whichever religion they are following. When Jesus said "the kingdom of God is within you," was He not talking about our Spirit, our Higher Self? And what do we hope to find in "the kingdom?"

In order to be aware and stay connected to our Higher Self, it is very important to spend as much time in solitude, as possible, thereby being able to clearly hear that "still small voice," inside our head. And with the hustle and bustle of the modern world, where noise constantly surrounds us, getting alone in nature, whenever possible, is one of the best ways of being in solitude. But when it isn't possible to go to nature, then a quiet place in your home is the second-best place to be in solitude.

The Lakota Sioux Indigenous Nation has a very important slogan: 'Mitakuye Oyasin: All my relations.' That is a far cry from our little comfort zone where we think of only our immediate family and friends. "All my relations" includes all of the animal nations and all of Creator's creation. The Indigenous people recognized, long before the invasion of the first Europeans on Turtle Island (North America) that the animals, forest, streams and all in their environment was part of their 'family,' and not just their biological family. And with all that is going on in the world today with wars, famine, climate change, etc., it could be the greatest blessing for mankind, if we all could embrace the concept of Mitakuye Oyasin, and apply it in our lives.

The healing philosophy of our Traditional Indigenous Nations versus Western medicine lies in the Spiritual aspect recognized by the First

Nations people of the Americas. As we all know, our modern western medicine focuses primarily on the physical body, and rarely acknowledging the importance of the mind and Spiritual components. And therefore, the physician typically treats only the physical body with drugs. The Lakota, as well as most Traditional Indigenous people believed that every living being on earth is a relative, and that their connection to all of the 'relatives' spirits nurtures their well being. This should behoove us all to understand that we are much more than just our physical body, and the proper "chain of command" is: Spirit-mind-body, and in that order, and not the other way around. Thus, the important understanding that we are a Spiritual being, merely having a physical experience on Planet Earth. With prayer and meditation in solitude is where we can all bring this concept into fruition for the betterment of all creation.

Spending as much time alone in nature as I possibly can, I have observed the hawk, eagle, coyote, fox, pronghorn, deer, elk, snake, rat and many other animals in their natural environment, and in their solitude I have witnessed how perfectly they live in harmony and balance with all other living things, without gathering together in large groups, as the humans often do, creating chaos, disruption and sadly, killings and wars.

If there was a blueprint or template for humans in how best to live in harmony and balance with our Sacred Earth Mother and all of Creator's creation, my suggestion for all of humanity would be to follow the Traditional Indigenous peoples' ways of being and living. My TRADITIONAL INDIGENOUS WAYS OF BEING documentary film can now be viewed on

YouTube, and it features my great Apache friend, Geronimo Vela and Washoe friend, Dr. Lisa Grayshield.

For those of us who have studied the history of the invading, first Europeans into the Americas, we learned that North America was a virtual "Eden," before the invaders began stealing the land of the Indigenous, forcing their religion on the natives, and killing and colonizing them. Could we dare imagine what our country might be like today, if the invading Europeans had embraced the lifestyles of the First Nations people, and learned to live in harmony and balance with them and with our Sacred Earth Mother and all of creation? I highly suggest that we consider that as 'food for thought.'

Today, some of our First Nations, Traditional Indigenous people have gone back to living in nature, as best they can, away from the noise, chaos and machinery of the modern world. And they are teaching their children how to live- in solitude and off the land, without all the trappings of modern society. One great Indigenous example is the Washoe Nation of Nevada and California. They are honoring and respecting their Sacred Earth Mother, and they are learning the very important lesson in life that "less is more!" By detaching and separating themselves, as much as possible, from Dominant Society, they are living a much more peaceful life in balance and harmony with nature, and embracing solitude at every opportunity, because they have realized the important and miraculous gifts they receive from Spirit when spending time in solitude with nature.

****

The world-famous Albert Einstein once said, "I think 99 times and find nothing. I stop thinking, swim in silence, and the truth comes to me.... The more I learn of physics, the more I am drawn to metaphysics." And some may ask, "What is metaphysics?" And the answer is this: It is a philosophy of being beyond the realm of the physical dimension. While physics deals with the laws that govern the physical world, metaphysics describes what is beyond physics – the immortal soul, the origin and nature of reality itself, and the existence of a Supreme Being. And again...when a person is able to spend time alone in solitude, that is where we are best able to experience, appreciate and enjoy the attributes of the metaphysical realm. For example, whenever I am writing a book, such as this one, I call upon my Spirit Guides of Love and Light to guide me in all that I do with love and light, and they assist me. The Guides exist in the metaphysical realm.

****

Photographing scenes in nature and sharing those images on social media with the world is an important and rewarding part of my life. One year recently, while on a five-day camping trip at the end of September in the High Country of southwest Colorado, a friend and I was traveling in a primitive wilderness area, and as my friend drove the vehicle, I was photographing beautiful landscape scenes. It was during the last morning of our trip, and my Nikon camera's battery had died, and in order to get just one more shot, I had been able to take the battery out of the camera, and by rubbing it vigorously on my pant leg, to reenergize it, I was able to get just one more shot, and the battery died again. I had been doing this routine throughout the morning hours, and since we had three more hours left before we each had to return home, my friend back to Denver, Colorado, and I back to Las Cruces, New Mexico, a hawk had appeared to me at this time outside my passenger side window, and I knew the significance of the hawk's appearance, as a guide and messenger to me. Being frustrated that I was unable to get more photos taken with my camera, while we were in a location with abundant and beautiful autumn foliage, I decided to call upon my Spirit Guides of Love and Light to assist me in recharging my battery. I asked my friend to stop the car and pay close attention to what I was about to do, and he could be my witness to the results. I took the dead battery out of my camera, held it in my right hand, and getting into a meditative state and summoning my Spirit Guides, via my third eye, I saw the head and shoulders of my deceased cousin, Mary Ann Russell, and she was smiling and nodding her head at me. I said to my witness-friend, "Okay, Rafael…you have seen me and I've told you all of the process, so now I am going to put the battery back into my camera, and if I get more than one photo with the inserted battery, you will be the witness to what happened." I inserted the battery, and as he slowly drove down the dirt road, and occasionally stopping for me to get out and take photographs, not only did I get more than one photograph, but I photographed for the next three hours, getting a hundred or more, and when I returned home that night, the battery still had enough charge that I was able to download all my photos onto my laptop computer. So, yes...my Spirit Guide heard me and responded to my need! And I thanked her. A'ho!

****

In solitude you may wish to think about what is most important for you to do with and in your life. For anyone that desires to get on the Red Road- the Indigenous Spiritual Road, I would highly recommend getting in tune with our Sacred Earth Mother, and that should begin with respecting her and all other living things on her bosom. By drilling into her body for oil and cutting her hair- the trees, which provides us with oxygen to breathe and stay healthy, we are destructive and destroyers as a species. And now, this present day, she is giving us very dire warnings about our future existence on her bosom. The extreme climate change globally is only getting worse and worse each new year, and it will, no doubt, lead to more viruses, diseases, famines, floods, heat waves, etc..

Who today is teaching their children: RDRU=Respect, Discipline, Responsibility and Understanding? If some parents and educational institutions are doing so, then I honor them greatly, because RDRU appears to have been missing in our society of humans for the past few generations. And for someone to understand the best way to learn and apply RDRU in their personal life and in the lives of others, the best answers can come to you by calling upon your Spirit Guides of Love and Light, followed by, spending as much time alone in solitude, as possible, in order to receive the messages.

Shall we dare imagine what could possibly happen in our halls of Congress in Washington, D.C., if all the members there would follow the simple directions that I have suggested above? What we presently have in our U. S. government is not working for the betterment of the country and its people. It is past time that they all, from the president on down to our town mayors, be reminded of who they are, first and foremost! They are servants of the people! If the media would begin using that label for them, perhaps it could cause a positive paradigm shift in our halls of government. There is too much power-playing, greed, lobbying, self-centeredness and uncaring people in Washington government, as it presently is. But when some of the early Europeans arrived on Turtle Island (North America), they recognized the good traits of the Iroquois Confederacy's form of government, and applied some of what they saw to the early American government. Said to have formed between 1570 and 1600, the Iroquois Confederacy consisted of the Mohawk, Oneida, Onondaga, Cayuga and Seneca Nations.

There should be little doubt that quietude and solitude played a big part in the Iroquois Confederacy being able to form a type of balanced and good type of government, because of a lack of confusing and disruptive noise and chaos in their lives. But contrasting that with today, we have excessive, human-made noises from trains, vehicles, whistles, technology, unruly crowds of people and on and on. We have all heard about the variety of pollutants upon our Sacred Earth Mother, but one pollutant is seldom, if ever, mentioned, and that is NOISE POLLUTION! And one 'noise pollution' throughout our country is the noises of people's dogs excessively barking, especially disrupting and irritating many of our sick and elderly people. But…. dogs are not the problem, the problem is the owner of dogs and other animals; owners that do not properly care for, control and discipline their animals, thereby, disrespecting their neighbors that are bothered by the uncontrolled and uncared-for animals.

When a person is able to learn about all of the benefits they can receive by being in solitude, they should be able to control their animal's noises, and realize many other benefits in their lives and other's lives from being in solitude. It is in solitude where we hear the infamous, 'still small voice,' and that alone time in solitude is when our instinct and intuition about a person, place, or thing can be most readily realized.

IN SOLITUDE

ED BREEDING

IN SOLITUDE   ED BREEDING

IN SOLITUDE   ED BREEDING

IN SOLITUDE   ED BREEDING

Chapter 3

It has been said that the invisible world is much more real than this physical world where our Higher Self-Spirit is housed in a physical body. I have had numerous experiences with the Spirits in their higher dimension of existence. Previously I mentioned about calling on my Spirit Guides of Love and Light to help me with my dead camera battery, and one came and recharged my battery, whereby I was able to take a hundred or so more photos. And you may ask, if that wasn't something sort of trivial, but no…the Spirits are aware of what happens in this physical dimension, and my deceased cousin that came to me that morning in Colorado knew how important my nature photography was, that I would be sharing the beauty and magnificence of our Sacred Earth Mother with the world, because

I always share my nature photos online to anyone and everyone that wants to see and enjoy them. Some of my photos have had over a thousand people liking them when two or three of the photos have been posted on social media. And many of those people have commented about how much they enjoyed and loved the photos of nature. My deceased cousin that came to me that morning in Colorado was a phenomenal poet, and I have included many of her poems in my 18 books, and in some of my 21 documentary films, because after her physical death, her husband gave me the rights to use any and all of her poems, as I saw fit, and in doing so, it has been a way for me to share her great work with the world. While living in Tennessee, whenever I created a major painting that I planned to release into a Limited-Edition Art Print, I would take the painting over to her house and spend the weekend with her and her husband. After spending time with the painting, she would write a wonderful poem about the painting, and I would include a copy of the poem with the sold art prints. Below is an example of her amazing poetry:

ANGELS UNAWARE

We side-step the panhandler whose down on his luck,
Or if someone is watching, maybe slip him a buck.
The kid down the street we've branded as wrong,
Cause his jeans are too tight, or his hair is too long.
A hungry child's wail we strongly resist,
And pretend the "Bag Ladies" don't even exist.
The ex-convict we ignore or evade,
Even though his debt to society is paid.
The prostitute we've already sentenced to hell,

And piously repeat each scandalous tale.
We look down our nose and jut out our chin
At the fellow who always smells strongly of gin.
We know that the Creator is all mercy and love,
So what could He ever have been thinking of?
When He dotted society with these wretched souls,
And left us to witness their misery and woes.
Could these be the angels He's placed with great care,
To judge our true nature as we entertain unaware?
                    ---MARY ANN RUSSELL

Mary Ann's poetry is such a great example of what a person is able to create in solitude, that I feel compelled to share one more of her poems with you! And although her physical body no longer exists, I am certain she is still aware of what I am doing with her important and wonderful poetry. And I'll forever be thankful to her and never forget her being able to recharge my camera battery when I wanted to photograph more of our beautiful nature scenes to share with the world.

MUSIC

How long I have existed no one could ever say.
I was here when the stars were cold, before the world was made.
I've walked the path of paupers, kept company with the kings,
I've climbed from prisons' pits of hell and soared on angels' wings.
I have seen the rise and fall of every civilization,
I dwell among the people of every color, creed, and nation.

I traveled with the angels to announce the Holy Birth,
Went hand in hand with the King of Kings as He walked upon the earth.
I've walked o'er bloody battlefields with strutting heroes brave,
And held the hands of cowards who fear a lonely grave.
I've been with the merry victors celebrating through the night,
Yet stayed and offered comfort to the ones who lost the fight.
I traveled with the astronauts who returned successfully,
I traveled with the ones who failed into eternity.
You'll find me with the mustang running free and wild.
Don't be surprised if I appear in the laughter of a child.

I help young lovers celebrate when happiness abounds,
When love goes wrong, I help them face a world turned upside down.
The red man found me often walking by his side.
I blessed his soul when all was lost, and kissed the tears he cried.
I was always in the Black man's heart, when the nights were dark and long,
Helped ease the chains of slavery when it seemed all hope was gone.
Tell the children all about me, make certain they all know,
I am far more precious than the world and all its gold.
In sunshine or in shadow, in Joy or in despair,
If ever they would need me, they'll find me waiting there.

But destruction will be sure to come if you ever should abuse me,
So people of this earth I pray, don't let the world misuse me.
I AM MUSIC...I AM FROM GOD!
    --MARY ANN RUSSELL

Mary Ann was born and raised in the mountain region of East Tennessee and Kentucky, and she only had a high school education, ah, but...she was so very connected to her Higher Self and our Sacred Earth Mother, whereby she saw and understood things about people and life, that very few people having Masters or Ph.D degrees could ever understand and know about the things that she knew and felt deeply about. And yes, she definitely spent a lot of sacred time IN SOLITUDE!, in order to create her "MASTERPIECES."

IN SOLITUDE   ED BREEDING

Chapter 4

The following are some famous people's quotes about being in solitude, which I find to be a very important contribution to this book:

"The best thinking has been done in solitude."

-Thomas A. Edison

"All man's miseries derive from not being able to sit quietly in a room alone."

---Blaise Pascal

"Conversation enriches the understanding, but solitude is the school of genius."

--- Edward Giggon

"People who take time to be alone usually have depth, originality and quiet reserve."

---John Miller

"Solitude is the great teacher, and to learn its lessons you must pay close attention to it."
>
> --Deepak Chopra

"The more powerful and original a mind, the more it will incline towards the religion of solitude."
>
> --Aldous Huxley

"I think 99 times and find nothing. I stop thinking, swim in silence, and the truth comes to me. The more I learn of physics, the more I am drawn to metaphysics....Be a loner. That gives you time to wonder, to search for the truth. Have Holy curiosity. Make your life worth living."
>
> ---Albert Einstein

"Come into the silence of solitude and the vibration there will talk to you through the voice of God."

---Paramahansa Yogananda

"Solitude is for me a fount of healing which makes my life worth living. Talking is often torment for me, and I need many days of silence to recover from the futility of words.... The journey is a great adventure in itself, but not one that can be talked about at great length. What you think of as a few days of Spiritual communion would be unendurable for me with anyone, even my closest friends. The rest is silence! The privilege of a lifetime is to become who you truly are. Your visions will become clear only when

you look into your own heart. Who looks outside, dreams; who looks inside, awakes."
>---Carl Jung

"In stillness lives wisdom. In quiet, you'll find peace. In solitude you'll remember yourself."
>--Robin Sharma

"I think it's very healthy to spend time alone. You need to know how to be alone and not be defined by another person."
>--Oscar Wilde

"Solitude helps you find peace. Peace helps you find happiness."
>–Maxime Lagace

"In solitude, the mind gains strength and learns to lean upon itself."

--L. Sterne

"I love to be alone. I never found a companion that was so companionable as solitude."
--Henry D. Thoreau

"In solitude is healing. Speak to your soul. Listen to your heart. Sometimes in the absence of noise, we find the answers."
–Dodinsky

"Solitude, in these days as much as ever, is an absolute necessity."
--Leo Babauta

"In solitude, one finds only what he carries there with him."
–J. R. Jimenez

"In the solitude of your dreams grows the flame that will bring the light to this world."
>--Anonymous

"Solitude will teach you how to navigate your inner dialogue. In the space of silence, you hear clearly, the voice of your own soul."
>--Nikki Rowe

"Talent is nurtured in solitude. A creation of importance can only be produced when its author isolates himself, it is a child of solitude....One can be instructed in society, one is inspired only in solitude."
>-J.W. Von Goethe

"Without great solitude, no serious work is possible."
>--Pablo Picasso

"Writing is utter solitude, the descent into the cold abyss of oneself."

--F. Kafka

"Solitude makes us tougher towards ourselves and tender towards others. In both ways it improves our character.... I hate who steals my solitude, without really offering me in exchange company..... I go in solitude so as not to drink out of everybody's cistern."

--Friedrich Nietzsche

"Listen to silence. It has much to say."

-Rumi

****

I expect that many of you may have read Henry David Thoreau's book: WALDEN. The following are some contents from that book which deal with what he achieved by being in solitude, and part of it is a personal declaration of independence, social experiment and voyage of spiritual discovery, and to some degree, a manual for self-reliance. He made scientific observations of nature, as well as metaphorical and poetic uses of natural phenomena. Thoreau went to Walden Pond to escape what he considered, 'over-civilization,' and he was in search of the 'raw' and 'savage delight' of the wilderness. By immersing himself in nature, Thoreau hoped to gain a more objective understanding of society through personal introspection, and simple living and self-sufficiency were his other goals. He spent two years, two months, two days at Walden Pond living a simple life without support of any kind. He said, "I went to the woods because I wished to live deliberately, to front only the essential facts of life, and see if I could not learn what it had to teach, and not, when I came to die, discover that I had not lived. I did not wish to live what was not life, living is so dear; nor did I wish to practice resignation, unless it was quite necessary. I wanted to live deep and suck out all the marrow of life, to live sturdily and Spartan-like as to put to rout all that was not life….."

****

All of those great people spoke about the importance of solitude in their lives, and how solitude allowed them to see, experience and learn why being in solitude can greatly enrich everyone's life in a very fulfilling way. Many of us have read about such notables as Einstein, Yogananda, Thoreau, Frankl, Jung and others, but perhaps we did not realize how important solitude was to every one of them. Sharing their thoughts and statements in this book gives great credence to the book's title: IN SOLITUDE.

Can we dare imagine what life may have been like while spending three years in a Nazi concentration camp? Well…not only did Victor E. Frankl (1905-1997) from Vienna, Austria, spend three years there, and during that time he lost his wife, parents and brother, but…during his time in solitude, it afforded him time to think about man's existence and the deeper meaning of life. Frankl was a psychiatrist, philosopher and Holocaust survivor. His accomplishments in life were legion, but one must wonder, besides the pain and torment of spending three years in a Nazi concentration camp, how did that time being in solitude contribute to his amazing accomplishments and his contributions to the world?

IN SOLITUDE   ED BREEDING

IN SOLITUDE   ED BREEDING

IN SOLITUDE   ED BREEDING

Chapter 5

In solitude it is much easier to hear the 'still small voice,' and in solitude you can recognize and more easily and wisely use your instinct and intuition. The word 'instinct' comes from Latin, meaning 'to instigate' or 'to urge.' It's an impulse that makes us act without thinking. And it's also a behavioral mechanism that allows us to respond fast enough to survive in dangerous situations. In other words, it allows us to act without thinking beforehand.

And as for intuition, it has been used for centuries in spirituality, philosophy and psychology. Intuition refers to our ability to understand without conscious reasoning. It has been referred to as the 'sixth sense.' In essence, it means that we are able to see things in our mind's eye, rather than just with our eyes. Some have called it inner wisdom, or…a hunch. When using our intuition, it's important to use reason and evidence along with intuition. But with instinct, it's usually accurate because it's based on a person's natural reactions to stimuli. For example, if you see a car in front of you on the road that has been swerving from left to right, your instinct tells you to keep a good distance behind the vehicle, or to pass it if the opportunity presents itself. And with instinct you don't have to think about something, and then come to a conclusion, because it's based on unconscious thinking, whereas, with intuition, you think about something and conclude. Intuition tells us things that we can't necessarily understand; something like a gut feeling. But instinct is based on our common biology and experience, such as seeing something that is dangerous, and we run away from it. This experience is hard-wired into our brains because it's beneficial to our survival.

Both instinct and intuition are played out and best arrives at a conclusion when we are in solitude. Even though we may have an instinct or intuition about a person, place or thing, whenever we are in a crowd of people, or around distracting noises, that situation can affect our instinct and intuition in a very negative way. In solitude is where 'the magic' typically takes place.

****

Our North American Traditional Indigenous' cultures typically believes that Spirit is in all of Creator's creations, and whenever we are in solitude we can commune with those spirits, whether they are the spirit of a deer, elk, coyote, or any other animal, and also the trees, plants and other living things. If in doubt, the next time you are in a forest or wilderness setting alone, give it a try and see what happens. And if you become distracted by too many visual things, close your eyes and via the 'third eye,' maintain complete silence and pay close attention to the energy vibrations around you, and as a message from the 'still small voice' enters your head, pay close attention to how it affects your mind and body, and the message will not be coming by way of words, but with your instinct 'in gear,' you may have a sense of knowing or a feeling of understanding something that you were previously unaware of. You may want to talk to a tree, just as you would with a fellow human being, perhaps telling it what you think of it and how you feel in its presence, and you may also wish to ask it questions, and staying in solitude, pay close attention to your energy vibrations, and be aware of a particular sensation or emotional feeling you may begin to experience. Whenever

I am alone in nature and the hawk appears, which is very often, I talk to it, and it doesn't fly away if it is on a tree limb or electrical pole. Our voice and words have an energy vibration which the hawk or other living things are able to connect with, and they can distinguish between a negative vibration and a positive vibration.

****

Shortly after beginning to write this book, I was talking on the phone with my good Apache friend, Geronimo Vela at UCLA, who is instrumental in getting all of my books published via Kindle Direct Publishing onto Amazon, as well as being my go-to-guide with any problems I may have with technology. He suggested that I include some of my life experiences and how being alone in solitude had brought many of those experiences to a good and positive fruition. And the following story is a good example of that.

During the writing of this book, I check my messages a few times daily on social media, and doing so today, I had a message from a young friend in Louisiana who had never sent me a message about an Indigenous native, but today's message from him was an interesting story about the famous Lakota activist, leader and actor: Russell Means. It was a story about Russell's youth, and how a family member had impressed upon Russell the importance of all other living things on our planet being part of our family, and how that had affected his life.

When reading my friend's message, I quickly realized that this was another way that our Spirit Guides of Love and Light are there to guide and help us, whenever we ask for their guidance in love and light. And so…I decided to add it to this book's dialog: The first documentary film that I had ever entered into a film festival was accepted and shown at the Santa Fe International Film Festival in 2007. My documentary was called ECHOES FROM THE ANCESTORS. Pearl Means, the wife of Russell Means saw my film at the festival, and she approached me about doing a documentary about the matriarchy of the Dine People (Navajo), her people. I accepted her request for me to do the film, and she told me that it was important that I attend a private Sun Dance with Russell and others at Wind Cave, South Dakota for six days and nights. And when I asked Pearl why she felt it was important that I attend the Sun Dance, if the documentary would be about the Dine women leaders, and not the men. But she told me it was because of a talk which Russell would be giving at the Sun Dance about the importance of women, which would be needed in the film. And so, I agreed to drive two days from New Mexico to South Dakota and attend the event. But when I arrived there, Russell informed me and some others from Italy and Australia that we would be needed to be a part of the Sun Dance for four days, because not enough 'Indians' had come for the event. Agreeing to assist Russell and the event, we danced in the special built arbor for four to five hours each day, until his eldest son, Tatanka pierced on the fourth day. Although I was there to do filming, at Pearl's request, I had no idea that I would be dancing each day in an arbor we had pre-built, shirtless and shoeless, as Russell's son who was to be pierced on the fourth day, danced around the center pole in the arbor, blowing an Eagle bone whistle, and each evening, we men were all required to spend time together in the Inipi. Most may know the Inipi as the sweat lodge, but Russell was adamant about it being called by its proper name: Inipi. The entire six days and nights that I was there could make a complete story within itself, and it was another amazing and learning experience I will never forget. During my time there, after our dancing each day, along with my video camera I hiked up into a wilderness area and spent time in solitude to appraise and evaluate each day's activity.

****

With the North American Traditional Indigenous Nations, the drumbeat represents the heartbeat of our Sacred Earth Mother. One early morning I went for a hike in our local Organ Mountains here in Las Cruces, New Mexico. I had planned to do a ten to twelve-mile hike, but after only hiking for a couple of miles, I felt the inclination to lie down on Earth Mother and just feel her energy. Within a few minutes I began to hear drumming, and with my mind, I thought it was very early for someone to be doing ceremony nearby, and since there were no other cars parked at the trailhead, I wondered where and who could be drumming that morning. I sat up to see if I could determine from which direction the drumming was coming, but when I sat up, the drumming stopped. I thought that was odd, and so I lied back down on the ground, and within a few seconds, the drumming continued. At that point I got the understanding that our Sacred Earth Mother was honoring me with "her heartbeat." I was so elated and honored to have had that experience, I returned home without finishing my hike. A few years later, I was asked to do some filming at our local university of a Storytelling event. Many Indigenous people were in attendance, and when I had finished the filming, I was sitting near a married Indigenous couple from the Blood Nation in Canada. I told them about my mountain experience of hearing the drumming, and when I asked their opinion of what it was all about, they both replied, "It's your song." That reply had me thinking deeply for quite awhile, but I finally came to an understanding of what they meant, but it's a bit difficult to put into words. Basically, I took it to mean that I had a sincere and respectful connection to our Sacred Earth Mother, and the drumming was the confirmation of that spiritual connection; my song.

Although I live in the city limits, and there is frequently vehicle noise outside, because my house has block and stucco walls, it is typically quiet inside, and that affords me an ample amount of time to go into solitude, think and write, paint, or prepare for my next documentary film. But it is when I venture out into nature in the early morning hours before daylight, that is when 'the magic' most frequently happens for me. Almost every time that I am out and away from vehicles, noise, people and homes, I see a hawk nearby, and most of the time it allows me to spend time with it and photograph it. And yes…I do talk to them softly, but not always in an audio voice.

In solitude, again…we can hear, see and know things that most others cannot. And since we are spiritual beings, merely having a physical experience here on Planet Earth, those entities from the higher frequencies and spiritual dimensions can connect and message us, and we can receive their messages via our third eye connection…when we are alone in solitude and receptive. But sadly, I have observed many people who are afraid to be alone and in solitude, and they prefer people and noise around them, whether it's the noise of a bustling city, or the loud noise of a radio or television, it doesn't seem to matter. One time in years past when I was visiting family members back east, I was talking to my brother in their living room, and the television was on and disrupting my ability to converse with my brother properly, and I asked if he could please turn the television off, and when he did, shocked... his wife came running into the room and asked what happened, and when he told her that I wanted to be able to talk with him in silence, she shrugged her shoulders and returned to her bedroom, perhaps hoping that I would soon leave, whereby she could have the noise back, which was in her comfort zone. I have chosen to include this particular scene in the book to illustrate how many, or maybe most people's home-settings are surrounded with noise, a noise which does not allow for great and effective communication, compared to when there is silence and solitude, which is not disruptive.

I suppose most of us have been invited to a gathering or social event where we have met someone for the first time, and we found ourselves so interested in what they had to say and share, that we wished we were somewhere alone with them in a quiet place, whereby we could have a wonderful and informative conversation, but in the midst of other people talking it would be difficult to fully appreciate the conversation. And although we may not be cognizant of the importance of silence and solitude at that very moment, our Higher Self-Spirit always remembers and knows the importance of silence and solitude. There have been times when I have been alone with another individual, and with respect, honesty and genuine care, our conversation has taken on such a depth that thoughts and words come to our minds, which we share with one another, that we never previously had such informative, amazing and refreshing thoughts. I came to realize that whenever that happened, it was our Spirits, our Higher Selves communicating with one another.

I have previously spent upwards of forty years of my life in Organized religion, and later I came to realize that there was one very important and major thing that I had never heard a preacher, reverend, priest, or any church leader talk about and discuss with the congregation, and that important thing was: who we really are, first and foremost; a Spiritual being...merely having a physical experience. And wondering why they never discussed and talked about that with a congregation, I came to realize that they may not realize it themselves, even thought their Holy Bible that they frequently hold in their hands makes it very clear, when Jesus said, "The kingdom of God is within you." And that kingdom is our Higher Self, our Spirit...our true identity.

And on a sadder note, while writing about Organized religion, one of the most memorable sermons I recall ever hearing was in Chattanooga, Tennessee when Pastor Ben Haden's sermon was titled: GARBAGE CAN CHRISTIANS. And his definition of a Garbage Can Christian was when someone picked something up off the ground, put it into their mouth, chewed on it and then spat it out, and you come along and pick it up and take that as "the Gospel," then you are a Garbage Can Christian. The reason that particular sermon resonated with me so much was because many of the people that I knew at that time never read or studied in solitude about the important issues in life, but instead waited for someone else to tell them what they had read and thought. During that same time I had read a book that I thought was very good, enlightening and informative, and a good friend asked about it, and I gave the book to him to read, and over a month later I asked him what he thought of my book and his response was, "Oh, I've only read the first page of the book. Tell me what it's all about." But I did not tell him what it was all about, I told him he must read it for himself, or he would miss out on a great lesson in life…but he never chose to read the book. And so it has been for many people that I know.

In our present-day-world where technology seems to control a large percentage of people's lives, they carry around a so called "Smart Phone," and constantly pushing its buttons, that becomes their primary source of information and "communication," and I have noticed that without that phone to connect with, many of our younger people today are unable to carry on an intelligent conversation, without their phone to feed them the answers or information. And so I ask, if the phone is the 'smart' one, then what does that say about the person that is constantly dependent on it for most of the things in their lives?? An anecdote for that sad situation might be for that person to occasionally go into solitude with a good book that a great author from the past, such as Paramahansa Yogananda, author of MAN'S ETERNAL QUEST and AUTOGIOGRAPHY of a YOGI, has painstakingly written about important and informative issues that can enrich our lives tremendously, if... we will only take the time alone in solitude and devote that time to enriching our lives by way of someone's information and experiences, whereby we can learn and grow from it. I recently heard a report that 40% of our U.S. population between ages 14 to 74 could only read up to a sixth-grade level. That was the saddest news I had heard in quite awhile.

****

While I was making a documentary film in 2009 in the Yucatan Peninsula of Mexico with the Mayan and Aztec people, about their ceremonies, rituals and sacred events, called REIGN OF THE JAGUAR, which now can be viewed on YouTube, two Mayan elders had this to say in the film: "It is imperative that mankind find a balance between materialism and spirituality, or he will self-destruct. There have been three (or four) previous humanities, that were technologically more advanced than we are today, and they self-destructed, and this present humanity is on that very same path of self-destruction." The Hopi Nation here in the North American west has the same thing to say in their prophecies. And constantly today, we are bombarded by extremes of climate change, whereby our Sacred Earth Mother is giving us dire warnings to change our ways, but... we are constantly disrespecting and abusing her, and in return we are getting extreme heat waves, droughts, flooding and other severe weather patterns, which our scientists say are only going to get worse, unless we immediately change our abusive, destructive, disrespectful and uncaring ways toward our Sacred Earth Mother and all living things.

I have frequently had people tell me about their personal problems in life, which they are unable to resolve by typical means, and I have suggested to them that they may want to go alone somewhere in solitude and have communion with their Higher Self, and by doing so, the Spirit realm may be ready to give them the answers and solutions to their problems which they have not been able to find answers for elsewhere. This present book that I am writing will be number 19, and alone in solitude, before writing, I call upon my Spirit Guides of Love and Light to assist me, and I have never been disappointed in their guidance and help.

A couple years ago I was driving alone on a rough, dirt road in the Sacramento Mountains of New Mexico. I had traveled on that road many times and hiked in the forests there, but that particular time I had driven farther than I had ever been previously, and the road was so remote and far away from a main highway, I realized that I needed to turn around and go back. But instead of driving on further where there may have been a decent place to turn around, I chose to back up on a hard dirt embankment to turn around, but when I did so, my car bottomed out on the top of the embankment, and…I was stuck! I couldn't drive out. My tires were spinning when I tried to drive out, and there were no other people in the vicinity to help me. After a brief panic-moment, I decided to call upon my Spirit Guides of Love and Light and Guardian Angel. Almost immediately I got a 'subliminal message' to open the trunk of my car and look inside. And inside my trunk I found a pair of heavy-duty Military knee pads, which I did not remember having. I immediately took them out of the trunk of my car and placed each of them at the edge of my front tires. I got back into my car, turned on the key, put the car gear into drive and pulled out very easily and smoothly. No problema! That is just another example while being alone in solitude and a problem may arise, by thinking clearly and listening to "the still small voice," so called…miracles can happen. I have learned to never include the words: fear or worry into my lexicon, because they carry with them a negative energy vibration. And although on that particular day I did have a brief moment of panic, the situation was quickly resolved in a great and memorable manner.

Another noteworthy metaphysical experience I had was when a Reiki Master with over twelve years of experience, from British Columbia, Margaret Dexter offered a free Reiki therapy in Chattanooga, Tennessee on a Sunday afternoon. I had previously read Barbara Ann Brennan's book, HANDS OF LIGHT, about healing through the Human energy field, and curious about Reiki, I and a nephew attended her event.

Two of her previous students where there, and they took my nephew to another room to Reiki him, and Margaret asked me to lie down on a cot in the living room where she would work on me. She began by telling me that she would call upon our Creator and Spirit Guides of Love and Light to come and assist her, and she told me I could do the same, if I liked, and I did. In Reiki, the practitioner does not physically touch your body as she scans your chakras-energy centers with the palm of her hands. Margaret was about three-fourths through her process when two 'Entities' came, and one 'Entity' grabbed my ankles with two hands, and another laid a hand firmly on my right shoulder, and their physical contact with me lasted a few minutes. All during the Reiki procedure, I kept my eyes closed. I was in a very peaceful and contented mood. When the two 'Entities' made physical contact with me, I was not concerned, and with my eyes remained closed, I thought that Margaret had called upon her two students to come and assist her, even though I knew that they shouldn't be making physical contact with me. After two or three more minutes, Margaret was at my left shoulder, and she said she was through with her procedure, but that I should lie there another minute or so before getting up, as I might be a little light-headed. When Margaret walked away, the two 'Entities' detached from me. I had my eyes closed during the entire process, enjoying the procedure, but I was curious as to what Margaret had found with my energy centers, but I was not afraid or concerned. When she told me that all my energy centers were functioning fine and properly, I asked about her two 'assistants' coming over to help her, and her response to me was shocking, when she said, "I was the only one with you physically, and whatever else you experienced, you'll have to deal with that." I asked if that was a common experience with her patients, and she replied, "In all of my years doing Reiki, you are only the second person that has told me of having that experience." Again…I was shocked, but elated!

While driving back home and telling my nephew of the wild experience I had with the two Entities making physical contact with me, when he asked what I thought it meant, I told him that I knew what it meant: the Spirit Guides of Love and Light made physical contact with me to prove to me beyond a shadow of doubt that they truly existed. And fortunately, I had been studying metaphysics for the previous number of years, searching for answers to questions beyond the physical realm, and the two Entities coming and physically touching me was my confirmation that they were real.

****

Another interesting metaphysical event that I will share with you, involved my amazing and wonderful, elderly neighbor lady, Polly Kelley, who lived in a home behind me here in New Mexico. Whenever I would complete one of my documentary films, I called to see if she would like to come over and see it, and excitedly, she always said, "I'll be there in fifteen minutes." She was always true to her word, and while watching my documentaries, she would sit forward on the end of the couch and become excited as one might be at a sports event. She often said, "Oh, my...I wish there would be more programs like this on television. It's beautiful and powerful!" She was always hunching forward on the couch as she spoke, and nodding her head.

Loving and dear, Polly passed away a few years later at the age of 92 or 93. Her daughter was now living alone in her house, and after completing my latest documentary, I told the daughter, Karen that her mother loved watching my documentaries, and I asked if she would like to come and see my latest one, and she agreed to come over and watch it. My sister and her daughter from Tennessee were visiting me at the time, and the four of us were watching my documentary in my living room. Suddenly I had a strong feeling that Polly's spirit was hovering over the television at the top of the ceiling. 'Telepathically' I asked her to do me a favor, and I also told her that what I wanted her to do was tacky, but, nevertheless, if she was really in the room with us, would she please take her daughter's right hand and rub her face or touch her hair, or something to do with her daughter's right hand, and then I would know beyond a shadow of doubt that she –Polly, was really with us.

    Karen was sitting on my couch where her mother always sat, but Karen was very quiet and reserved, and in no way showed excitement about my film like her mother had always done when she watched one of my documentaries. My niece from Tennessee was also sitting on the other end of the couch, near me in my recliner chair.

I glanced back at the ceiling where I had felt that Polly's spirit was hovering, and I began to count the seconds as I glanced back at Karen who was sitting very quietly on the couch watching my film. I thought for a moment to myself that I was being silly, but as I counted to seven seconds, Karen's right hand crudely reached up and began scratching her cheek briskly, as a monkey might do it. And then her hand went back down to her lap, but there was no emotion or any type of reaction on Karen's face, as the event took place. I was stupefied, and I grabbed my niece's arm and told her to follow me outside to the back yard. We rushed outside, and I told her what happened. She was shocked, but said she never noticed anything happening with Karen. I didn't tell Karen that day, but the following day I walked over to her house and told her what happened, and she responded, "Ed, I don't recall rubbing my face with my right hand." I told her that it was her mother that did it, and to my dismay, she wasn't very surprised, as she told me that she always talked with her mother every day after her passing.

That true story was another example as to what can take place in our lives when we learn to spend time in solitude, alone with the Angels and Spirit Guides of Love and Light, which I often do. It can prepare us to be ready for such an event that I just shared. And it's another reminder of what I learned many years ago, that the Invisible world is much more real than this physical world, which has been referred to as a dimension of illusion or maya.

****

I do believe in reincarnation, and that many of us have had previous lives on other planets. In October of 2000, while living in Dayton, Tennessee, a cousin asked me to accompany her to a Psychic Fair in Chattanooga, Tennessee. I had never been or had an interest in such an event, but I went with her anyway. As I walked around the fair, nothing there caught my attention, until I saw a tall, slim woman with long black hair standing alone near the edge of a forest area. I was drawn to her, and I walked over to meet her, and we had a great conversation. She was from North Carolina, but she was staying the following week at a friend's house in town, and I decided to let her do a Past Lives Regression and Clearing on me the following morning at her friend's house.

Her name was Sha'La, and as I lied on a cot in the living room, with a recorder running, she began with the regression and clearing:

"…. you've been on other planets, too, you know. I do see Egypt. I'm asking my guides what that is in your head. I see a pyramid. I see you now, like in a couple different lifetimes; an Egyptian here and a, well…you're going back to Syria; the Dog Star constellation; the planet Cyrus or whatever. You were on the second group of ships which came to this planet. You came to inhabit the thought form of this energy field. You helped put in what was needed in the, uh…they call it a Keylock (lights?) of the underground. Even though the pyramid was up on top, it goes down, and if you take all the dirt away, it's a big diamond. And somehow, you and the group of people you were with were forming that lower-level chamber." The archeologists and those who have studied the lower chambers of the great Pyramid at Giza in Egypt may find this interesting.

That was an example of what the hour-long session entailed. There were many more interesting events that were covered in my life at that time, and some of them have since come to fruition, such as some of the people in one of my previous lives in England, and that I would be meeting when I moved to New Mexico, and...I have met them.

I began over thirty years ago reading and studying every book that I could find on metaphysics and the higher, Spiritual dimension of existence. It was as though I had a 'knowing,' or understanding that other higher dimensions existed, but I had never heard anyone talk about them, and I was very interested to find out about them, because I instinctually felt a connection. It was necessary for that all to take place in solitude. And the more I read and studied, the more eager I was to learn and 'AWAKEN' to what is.

Some of those books which helped me to "Awaken," were: *Autobiography of a Yogi* and *Man's Eternal Quest* by Paramahansa Yogananda. *Hinds Feet on High Places* by Hannah Hurnard. *The Prophet* by Kahlil Gibran. *Hands of Light* by Barbara Ann Brennan. *The 12th Planet* by Zecharia Sitchin. *The Power of Now* by Eckhart Tolle. *Anatomy of the Spirit* and *Sacred Contracts* by Caroline Myss. *A World Before* and *A World Beyond* by Ruth Montgomery, and…many more.

ELMENDORF AIR FORCE BASE ANCHORAGE ALASKA

IN SOLITUDE   ED BREEDING

Enchanted in Mexico

A mystical and breathtaking river ride

IN SOLITUDE					ED BREEDING

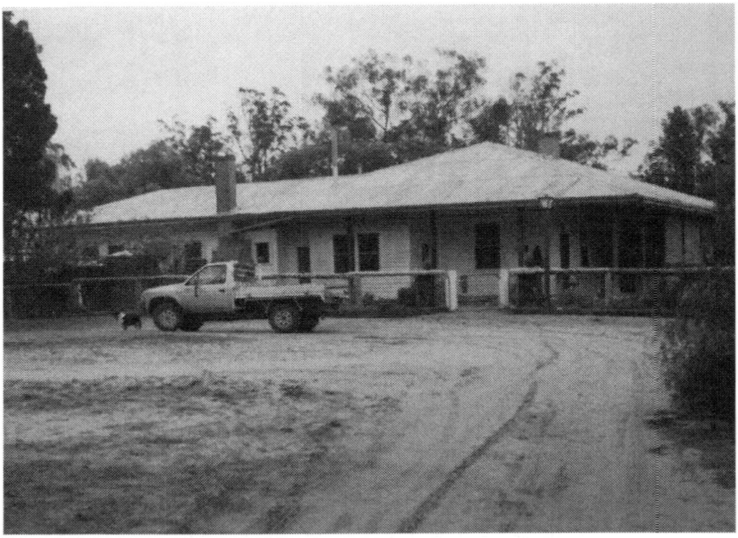

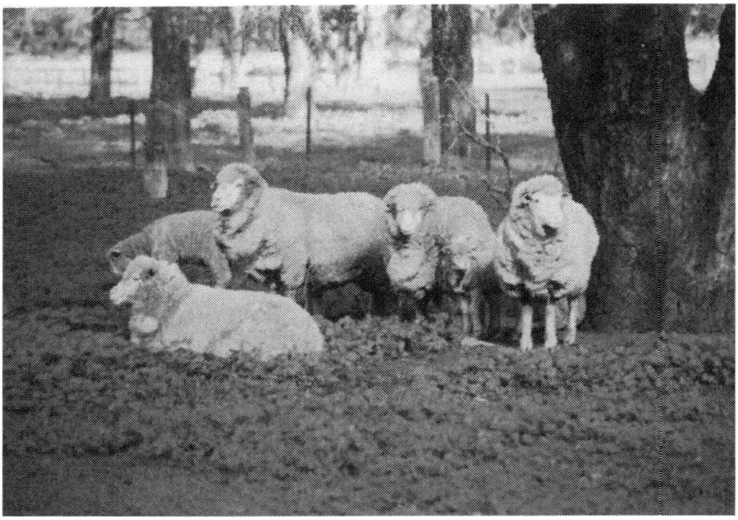

IN SOLITUDE   ED BREEDING

IN SOLITUDE ED BREEDING

IN SOLITUDE				ED BREEDING

Chapter 6

In our present day, in October of 2023, there are wars in the Middle East, Ukraine, Russia and 'fires and hatred' in the hearts of mankind around the world. That is all an example of human's disregard for our Sacred Earth Mother, who provides all of our physical needs, and our Creator's command to love thy neighbor as thy self. If the masses of humanity could only recognize that they are first and foremost a Spiritual being, merely having a physical experience, then perhaps there would never be another war. By recognizing our true identity and spending time in solitude with our Higher Self, plus knowing the important attributes of our Higher Self-Spirit, which are: love-peace-truth-compassion and understanding; and by fully recognizing these attributes, there would be no place left for hatred, greed, power-seekers, envy, jealousy and killings, because…we would realize that we are all part of the ONE, and connected to one another. But that understanding can only be achieved by each and every one of us spending time alone in solitude, whenever the opportunity presents itself.

While spending time alone in solitude, we are able to tap into a deeper and more spiritual understanding of all that is, and… how our Creator designed it to be! But that can never be achieved when we constantly surround ourselves with noise, unruly groups, games and unnecessary confusion, distractions and chaos.

It seems that most of us spend the bulk of our time in our "comfort zone," and that comfort zone typically includes the same small group of people and events, which may include only family members and a few friends; but in order to grow in a spiritual way as a human being, it is very important to expand that circle and apply the attributes of our Spirit on those special occasions with others, outside our little circle of a few.

After spending six years of my life in the U.S. Air Force, four years Active, and two years in the Reserves, I cherished the three full years of that time spent in Germany, where I was able to travel throughout Western Europe and into Northwest Africa. From those travels I learned about different cultures, and different ways of doing things. My hunger and appetite was piqued to learn and understand as much as I could about the world, and after my six years with the Air Force was fulfilled, I continued to travel in many different parts of the world as possible. But...I did not travel in groups or on tours, I traveled alone in solitude, as much as possible, and acquiring an International pen-pal group, which led me back to parts of Germany where I had never been, to the Basque Country in Spain, where I had never been, to Hungary, Australia, Cuba, Honduras, Costa Rica, Canada and, of course, Mexico. Throughout all of those countries, by traveling alone, and living with the people from those countries, I was greatly blessed to learn about their cultures, and... even get a much deeper understand of the USA, by seeing it through the eyes of someone from a different country. That was a great and important lesson for me. While in a bookstore in Spain, on the outside window was written these words: "The world is a book, and those that don't travel read only a page." --St. Augustine.

****

While in the U.S. Air Force Reserves at Dobbins Air Force Base in Georgia, near Atlanta, my group's two-week summer camp took place in

Anchorage, Alaska at Elmendorf Air Force Base. My group and I were working there in the Cargo terminal when an officer quickly learned that I was an artist, and so... Instead of working the two weeks in Cargo, he took me to town and we purchased all the art supplies that were needed for me to paint a 16 x 20 foot mural of Alaskan wildlife on a large blank wall in the Cargo terminal. I painted the brown bear, moose, salmon, wolf and some other animals relevant to Alaska. Although I went there with a group of fellow airmen, I was allowed a wonderful time to be alone in solitude as I created the huge wildlife mural, during the day and evening hours of my choosing. That was just another example of how important solitude can be in our life when we are ready and have prepared ourselves to be receptive to it. I was in the best of both worlds in that situation, and by that, I mean: I greatly enjoyed and loved the time spent in Alaska with my fellow airmen, but I also enjoyed and loved the alone time I was given to produce the large mural, which was greatly appreciated by the people there in the Cargo terminal. Another plus for me during my time in Alaska, an airman that was stationed there was so appreciative of my mural painting, he invited me to his home one evening where his Eskimo wife from Nome, Alaska prepared an amazing salmon dinner for us; and the airman had also built an amphibious vehicle where he spent a month each year on the tundra with it hunting moose, and he invited me to come up there and join him one year on a hunt. I was very honored by his invitation, and when I asked him about the dangers from brown bears, he told me, "I have seen upwards of fifty bears while on the tundra hunting, but I have never had a confrontation or problem with any of them. My life here has taught me to understand, respect and appreciate them, and they've left me alone and I've left them alone." This story is just one example of when we have spent time alone in solitude, and honed our creative gifts, other people often respond to our gifts in a great and wonderful way.

****

After leaving my managerial job in Tennessee and begin painting for a living, for the entire month of September in the 1990's I decided to drive up to Mt. Desert Island, Maine and rent a cottage on Southwest Harbor and paint every day on location; scenes of nature and interesting subjects there. Since lobster was the primary crustacean that the fishermen were after, I painted lobster traps and buildings, et cetera, as one subject, and then I would drive to a secluded bay with a boat house, and paint that scene. Another time I would paint the sail boats in the harbor. I typically completed a painting a day, and having the cottage all to myself, I had plenty of time in solitude to reflect and read up on the history of certain locations in the state of Maine. Bar Harbor was the only town on Mt. Desert Island, and an art gallery there took all of the location paintings that I had done, and put them up for sale, eventually selling all of them.

I took a couple days to tour interesting locations in Maine, such as Acadia National Park, and there I painted the ocean scenes and high rock bluffs. I was told that that area had one of the highest ocean tides of anywhere. It was a fascinating place to be and paint on location. Another time I drove to the northern part of Maine and visited Baxter State Park, and while hiking in the forest there I came upon a moose with a huge rack of antlers. It was a wonderful feeling to be alone in the wilderness with such an amazing and calm animal.

Before leaving Maine I spent a day in Camden, and from Camden Hills State Park I painted a couple scenes of the sail boats down in the harbor below me. But before leaving Maine, I must share with you my lobster experience at my cottage. I had purchased a live lobster and was told how to prepare it in a pan of boiling water, and as I did so, with it squirming around, after it was cooked…I could not eat it! It was the grossest cooking experience I had ever had. But…I did have lobster in restaurants a couple of times while in Maine.

****

I have always enjoyed the sound and rhythm of the Spanish language, and when I read of a Spanish Emersion Course being offered at the Forester Institute in San Jose, Costa Rica, after giving it much thought in solitude, I decided to go there for the three-week course. San Jose is the capital of Costa Rica, and during my time there as a student at the institute, I was required to live with a married couple of San Jose who did not speak English. They were wonderful hosts, and because they did not speak English, all of our conversations had to be in Spanish. Well…since the classes at the institute greatly involved conjugating Spanish verbs, I learned more about speaking Spanish by living with the Costa Rican couple than I did at the institute. I walked back and forth from my 'home' to the institute each weekday, and on weekends our class did excursion trips to interesting outlying areas. One weekend we explored a jungle setting with exotic birds and wildlife, a cloud forest and a butterfly farm, and another weekend we stayed at a resort near the Arenal Volcano, where at night we could see orange-red lava spewing from the top of the volcano. I did horseback riding in a hilly region behind the resort, and at night I could hear Howler monkeys in the nearby forest. We were told that a small town of over a thousand people had been buried beneath the volcano from a previous eruption, and now that area was covered by a lake. The Costa Rican trip was one of the most exciting and enjoyable foreign trips that I have ever taken, and very educational because of the fellow students who shared their life experiences with me, and especially the time I spent in a home with my wonderful and warm, host couple. And after returning home from that trip, one of my fellow students at the institute, who lived in New York City, came to visit me at my home in Tennessee, and we had a great time reminiscing about our time spent in Costa Rica.

So, yes…my world travel experiences have been a great education for me.

****

Becoming an independent documentary filmmaker is another one of the wonderful gifts that the Great Spirit bestowed on me, and about eight years ago a cousin hired me to fly to Vera Cruz, Mexico and film her Mexican boyfriend's daughter's quiencenera: the coming-of-age ceremony. The event took place in the small mountain town of Altotonga, and the boyfriend's family provided a family house for me to live in by myself, as the house's family members were away in the USA at that time. My time alone in solitude in the house allowed me to think and consider the best way to schedule my time there, whereby I could do the best job that I was paid to do. And the pay was only for my expenses. I did not charge my cousin for my filming. It was all another great and enjoyable learning experience, by living in the small family compound, and them all sharing their life experiences with me...yes, another education in traveling. Later we traveled to a jungle location and went horseback riding in the jungle, and for the first time in my life, I filmed video footage while riding my horse...a fantastic experience in the jungle. And on my final day there, since my cousin knew how much I loved nature, she took me to an amazing, crystal-clear river, and having my video camera with me, I decided to walk a couple miles up the riverbank and film different portions of it, and also film some young children playing and swimming in the clear water. I walked all the way to the headwater of the river, and there I filmed a magnificent waterfall that was flowing from a huge, pure spring above. Again, I did this all-in solitude, and the experience was magnificent.

When I returned home to New Mexico, I decided to make a short film of the river experience and I called it: ENCHANTMENT IN MEXICO.

****

I realize that many people travel to foreign countries, but often they are in groups, and often on tours where someone else is telling and showing them what to see and do, but how many of us are traveling alone, whereby we are able to have one-on-one interaction and conversations with people from other nations and cultures? And why are more people not traveling alone, whenever they have the opportunity to do so? May I suggest that the reason may be because of the "god" of the masses, and that god of which I speak is: FEAR! Fear of the unknown is one of mankind's greatest fears, but if the truth be known, the unknown is oftentimes where the adventure, learning and productive excitement lies in waiting for us to partake of it.

****

While visiting my newfound friend, Keith Sloane in New South Wales, Australia, and staying a week or so with him and some of his family on their Savernak Sheep Station, which consisted of 10,000 acres, where they raised Marino sheep, I learned about the sheep-wool business, the different kangaroos, and many other special things about how the people thought and felt about the world around them. I was also introduced to their 40-year-old cockatoo, which the family had since its birth. While there, a young woman from New Zealand was brought in to grade the sheep's wool. I observed how all the sheep that were to be sheared, were first run through a wooden trough filled with liquid disinfectant, before the sheep were sheared. I also observed the shearing process, and on the station, a married couple living in a small house away from the main house, they invited me to spend some quality time with them in their home, and besides working on the sheep station, the husband was a great musician, and he had previously played in bands across Australia, and sometime in New Zealand. He kindly gave me a private 'concert' of his music on their front porch. It was a spectacular and wonder-filled event, and the couple's genuine hospitality was unparalleled. They felt free to share their life experiences with me, and they were willing to answer any questions that I had for them. Money could not replace the warmth and love that I experienced with those people on Savernak Station. My previous times spent in solitude have prepared me to always share my true and authentic self with whomever I meet while traveling in the world, and like the hospitable couple above, it seems to always inspire them to be their true and authentic self.

An interesting experience when I first arrived at my friend Keith's home was: when I went to the bedroom that was prepared for me, it was cold, and getting into bed, the amount of quilts on the bed were so heavy that I didn't know if I would ever be able to go to sleep, but I did. And the following cold morning, I went into the bathroom to take a shower, and a window was left open. I immediately closed it before showering. And when I went into the kitchen where Keith was preparing our breakfast on a wood-burning stove, I told him that he had left the bathroom window open, but I closed it. He replied, "Ed, I left the window open so that fresh air could come in." The year I was there was in 2002, and I believe the month was August, anyway, it was wintertime in Australia. I remember the outside temperature was in the low 40's. And the only heat in Keith's large house was the kitchen cook stove. I said no more about the cold house, because I quickly recalled that where I lived the first ten years of my life in East Tennessee, the only heat we had in our home back then was wood burning stoves: a kitchen stove and a small pot-bellied stove in the living room-bedroom. No electricity and no running water. A nearby spring provided our fresh water, and our toilet was a one-hole outhouse. And so...while staying with Keith, I was able to relive part of my childhood, and I relished every minute of it.

Keith was a World-class Mountain climber, and being a nature-lover like myself, he also knew that I enjoyed snow-skiing, so he took me to a region near the famous Blue Mountains where he pointed out an area where the famous

Australian, Mel Gibson owned a large parcel of land. The ski slopes that day had mushy and wet snow, so I opted not to ski, and leaving the slopes, Keith drove me around the beautiful Blue Mountains, and we had a wonderful and enjoyable day. Keith enjoyed his solitude as much as I did, and so we were never in a large group of other people while I was with him.

After spending more time with Keith at his Savernak Station (ranch), I took a train up Australia's northeast coast, seeing large groves of bananas, and past the Great Barrier Reef, to the town of Cairns. There I got to see and learn a little about the First Nations people of Australia, the Aborigines. But sadly, what I saw and learned there was that some of them were still being treated like the first Europeans treated the First Nation's people of the Americas, upon their first arrival from Europe.

Of course, the northern part of Australia was tropical and warm, and I went with a group and spent a day in a jungle-type environment, and while there I saw and filmed birds and animals I had never seen or heard of before. We were also able to see the elusive platypus at the edge of a pond. The platypus is an egg-laying and burrowing, aquatic monotreme of Australia, having a duck-like bill. It is also called: duckbill. It's about two feet long with a tail about five and a half inches. I had heard of the exotic platypus, but I never dreamed of ever seeing one as it splashed around the edge of a small pond. And while on that exciting and educational tour, we were taken to a cascading waterfall, where we slid down from the moss-covered rocks at the top into a refreshing pool below, where leeches attached to our bodies. But, we easily pulled them off quickly. With our small group of six or eight, I met and talked with people from a number of European countries, who shared with me, many of their exciting world traveling experiences on a very low budget, and how they did it.

I never met any Americans during my time in Australia, but I did meet some traveling Europeans. And it was very refreshing to learn that they were there in the country from two to three months, staying mostly in youth hostels, or…with families where they worked on their 'stations', and received enough money to pay for their extensive travel expenses. That impressed me very much, especially since most Americans that I knew who traveled, spent more money in a day on their "vacations," than I and the Europeans did in an entire week or more.

From the tropical north of Australia, I traveled back south via a bus, and one of our stops along the way was in a small town whose claim to fame was a group of standing stones, which I visited as I hiked upon top of a secluded hill. Before going to Australia, I had been told that the people there were much like people were in the USA a hundred years earlier, and what I experienced in Australia, wherever I went was friendly, helpful, hospitable and warm people.

We had a few hours layover in the small town with the standing stones, and in the bus station/café, there was an interesting picture on the wall that I was observing, when a friendly gentleman walked up and asked if I knew what I was looking at, and when I said I didn't know, he replied, "Well, my good man, what you are seeing is a 'Pub Crawl,' and a Pub Crawl entails a group of mates riding on horseback from one pub to the next pub to a twelve mile or so village, and there we partake of another beer, before mounting our horses and riding into the next village and pub, having a beer, and on to another village pub and beer, and all taking up about a forty or more mile trip. And that's what's called a…Pub Crawl." Live and learn!

Still traveling alone by bus, I spent a night in a youth hostel in Melbourne, and the next morning I rode a bus to Sydney, where I visited the world famous, Opera House and the beautiful Botanical Gardens, before flying back home to the U.S. Although it was wintertime while I was in Australia, none of the hotels, hostels, or restaurants were heated, and when I asked why, I was told that they saved their money to be able to keep their homes cool in the hot Australian summers. And their answer to staying warm in the winter was to just wear more clothing, and more quilts and blankets on the bed.

My trip to Australia allotted me a lot of time in solitude, where I was able to reenergize and fully appreciate and enjoy the variety of experiences, people and locations that I visited. My three weeks in Australia, including travel expenses, hotels and food, probably cost less than many people spend on a week's vacation in the states. For example, the Youth Hostels I stayed in were only about twelve dollars a night, and not being a fussy or big eater, less than five dollars a day was spent on food. The highlight of my trip was spending quality time with the open-minded and candid people I met and had refreshing conversations with along the way.

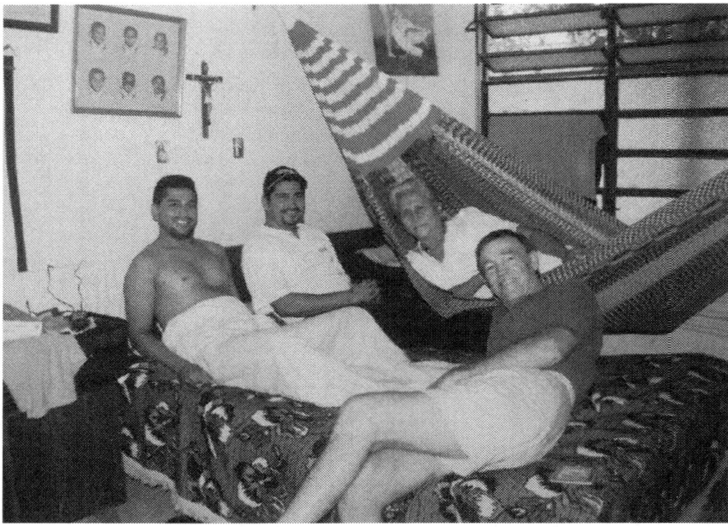

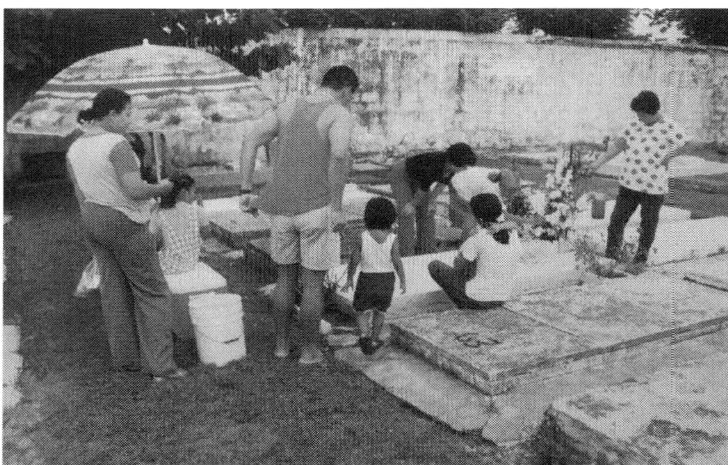

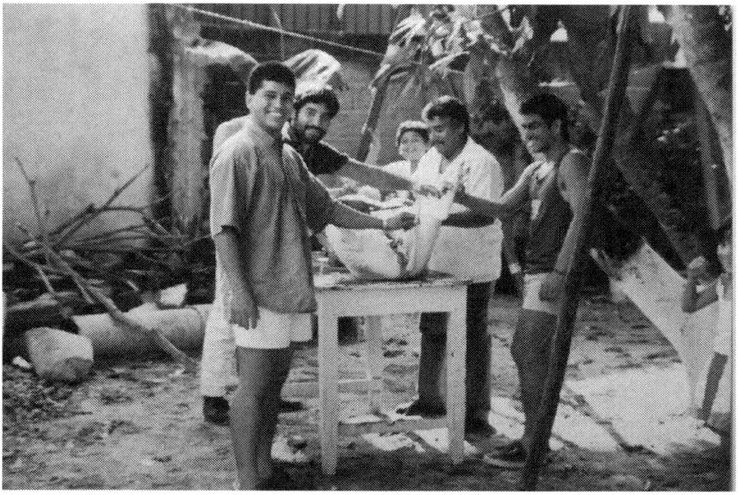

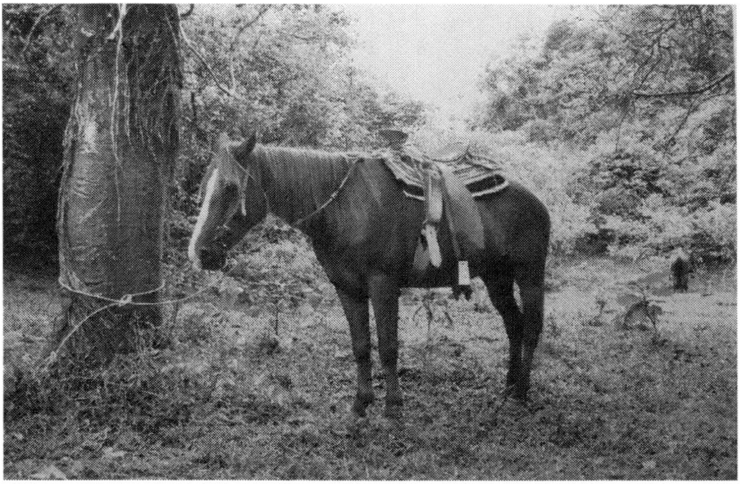

IN SOLITUDE   ED BREEDING

IN SOLITUDE ED BREEDING

Chapter 7

It was an accident that happened to me in 2002 which awakened me to make my international trips. While living in Dayton, Tennessee, where I had previously been Superintendent at the La-Z-Boy Chair Company, a roofer had begun to replace my house's roof. It was late in the month of October, and my concrete walkway in front of my house was icy. I had held my aluminum ladder for the roofer to go upon my roof, and then I proceeded up the ladder to join him. But when I reached the top rung of the ladder and stepped one foot forward onto the roof, the ladder slipped from beneath me and I fell backwards onto the cold and icy concrete below. My fall backwards appeared to me as if it was happening in slow motion, and what quickly ran through my mind was that I might die or live, but by having some martial arts classes in Germany during my time in the U.S. Air force, a split second before impact, I slammed my left arm onto the concrete to break the fall, and keeping my head and back from getting damaged in the fall. The roofer panicked and thought I had broken my back, but I quickly stood up and told him not to jump off the roof, that I was okay. The extent of my body damage from the fall was, I had knocked the fluid out of my left shoulder rotary cup, causing me to be unable to write or paint. I was left-handed, and after leaving the corporate world behind, I had been making my living by creating fine art paintings. I forced myself to learn how to 'primitively' write with my right hand, which I continue to write with today, because of a nerve problem in my left arm, but rather than sitting alone at home and feeling sorry for myself, I began my trips to foreign countries, and by doing so, I was able to fulfill my longing for learning about different people and cultures of the world. And one might ask how being in solitude played into all of that, and the answer is this: prior to each of the trips that I made during that recuperation time, in solitude I read, studied and planned my itinerary for each country that I visited, and by doing so, after returning home from all of those trips, I felt as though I had earned a 'Masters Degree' in International cultures and travel.

****

My long weekend trip to Havana, Cuba happened when I was staying with my good Aztec friend, Javier Alarcon and his family in Puerto Juarez, Mexico, just outside of Cancun. I had been washing my clothes down the street from his home in a public laundromat, and reading a newspaper there, I saw a weekend trip to Cuba was offered for a very low fare. Returning to Javier's home, I asked his wife what she thought about me going to Cuba, and since she had been there three times, she highly recommended it, and suggested I take their next-door neighbor, Enrique del Valle along with me. Enrique had been coming over each evening to visit me, and we had become close friends, and although he didn't speak English, we got by with the little Spanish that I knew.

The prop plane from Cancun to Havana was old and ragged, and the seat's armrests were torn and shabby, but...we arrived in Havana safe and sound. Our trip package-deal included the roundtrip flight, hotel and food. While eating a salad one evening I was surprised that the lettuce in my salad was wilted, but what I learned during my trip explained a lot about Cuba. The people were living in poverty, and I felt that the USA

Embargo on Cuba was to blame for much of the misery there.

While riding on a bus in town one day, I noticed a large group of people standing three abreast in a long line across the street, and when I asked a Cuban man on the bus what was going on with the large group of people, he said, "Oh, they're standing in line to buy an ice cream cone. And since the Cuban peso is almost worthless, if you have a Yankee dollar you can go to the front of the line and immediately get an ice cream cone." I was shocked and in almost disbelief that such a large group of people would be standing there for hours, just for a cone of ice cream.

Enrique and I were in Cuba during the time that the young Cuban boy named Elian Gonzales had been living in Miami with a relative, against the father's will. As I recall, the boy's mother had drowned during her and the boy's boat crossing to Miami. Enrique and I were walking around town one day and noticed a large event taking place on a plaza with hundreds of people present, and with flags flying. The event was the return of Elian Gonzales to his father in Havana. It was all big international news during that time.

Enrique's highlight of the trip was to purchase two boxes of the famous Cohiba, Cuban cigars, and he did. And on our last evening there we were walking back to our hotel, and because he was wearing new slippers, he had blisters on the heel of his feet, and he was walking slowly and far behind me when I saw an old, thin and weathered-looking woman sitting at the edge of the sidewalk with an old tin cup in her hand. Before getting close to her, I reached into my front pocket and got the largest Cuban coins I could find and dropped them into her cup. But when I did so, tears were in her eyes as she quickly grabbed my hand and began kissing it, not wanting to let go of me. I cried also, as I walked away, and I glanced back to see if Enrique had witnessed the touching event, but no…his head was bowed down, apparently in foot pain from each step that he took.

Enrique's day job in Cancun was as an electrician, paying only eighteen dollars a day, but after our trip in Cuba, he told me, in Spanish, that he thought Mexicans were very poor people, but after our experience in Cuba, he said that Mexicans were rich, compared to the people of Cuba. I thought he was being very insightful. Our Cuban experience was wonderful, educational and rewarding for us both. And when we returned to Mexico and sharing our Cuban experience with Javier and his family, they were very happy that we had had such a great and rewarding trip.

It was a couple years after our trip to Cuba that Enrique invited me to join him to visit his family living in Tabasco, Mexico. I accepted that invitation, and we had to travel by bus at nighttime because of the extreme heat in the daytime. The trip took twelve hours. His mother's home in Tabasco had no glass in the open windows, and hammocks were used as beds. I awoke early one morning from the squeal of a pig outside our bedroom window. Getting up to see what was going on, some of Enrique's relatives were butchering the pig on a concrete slab, and draining the blood into a bucket below, to be used by the mother to make a pudding from the pig's blood. And no…I didn't eat any pudding that feast- evening.

The del Valle family ran a tortillaria in their yard, and all the neighbors came there to purchase their daily tortillas. Enrique's mother was always up at five a.m. to begin starting up the gas-heated conveyer belt that slowly cooked the tortillas. They showed me the entire operation, and it was fascinating to watch as the tortillas moved down the conveyor belt, and at one end a child was placing the premade tortillas on the belt and at the other end someone was taking them off the moving belt and stacking them up in piles, and all during the day, customers were coming by to purchase the tortillas. I was treated like family in Tabasco, and later realized…they were family!

****

In the late afternoon before taking our night bus ride back to Cancun, Enrique's mother wanted us to accompany her and other members of the family to the cemetery where her husband was buried. The husband/father had died the previous year, and an altar was prepared for him in the dining room of their home. The mother asked that we each take a gallon of water with us to the cemetery. I thought that was an awful lot of water to be taking, just to drink, because we wouldn't be living there for a week, I thought, but the water wasn't for drinking! After arriving at the cemetery, the mother slowly and prayerfully poured each gallon of the water over the top of her husband's grave... in order to cool him off from the hot tropical sun. That was one amazing experience that I shall never forget. I felt so honored and fortunate to be accepted into Enrique's family as I was, and before leaving Tabasco, a couple of Enrique's relatives asked if I would return sometime and teach them English, and I said that I would consider it. I asked when the coolest time of the year was, and they replied that it was always hot there, and never got cool. Sadly, I never returned to Tabasco, Mexico to teach English.

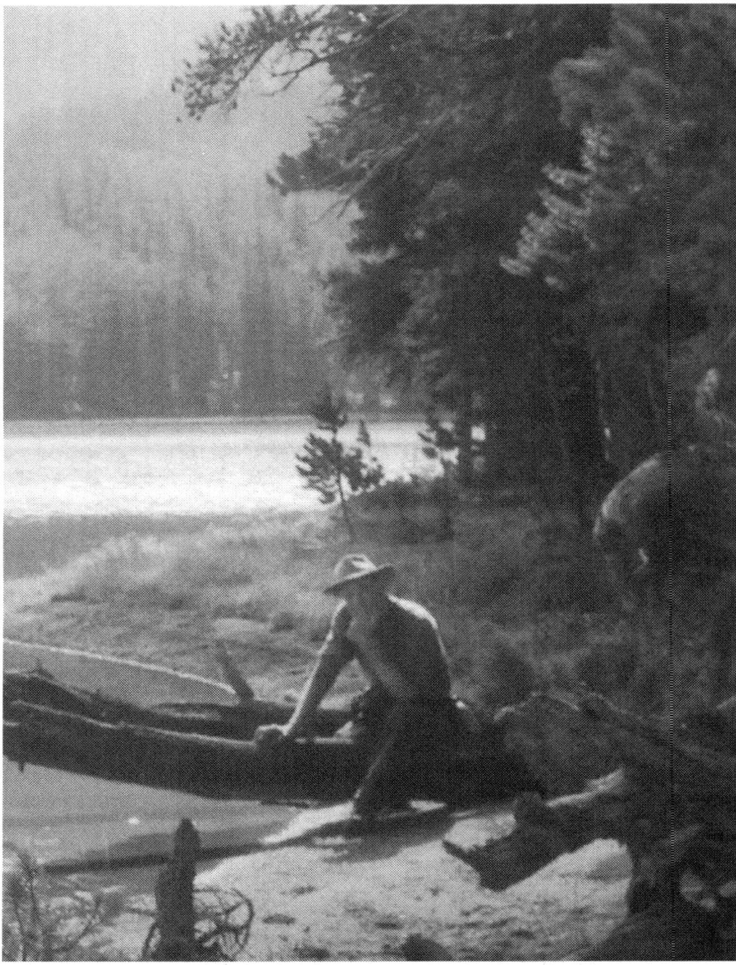

IN SOLITUDE   ED BREEDING

IN SOLITUDE — ED BREEDING

IN SOLITUDE ED BREEDING

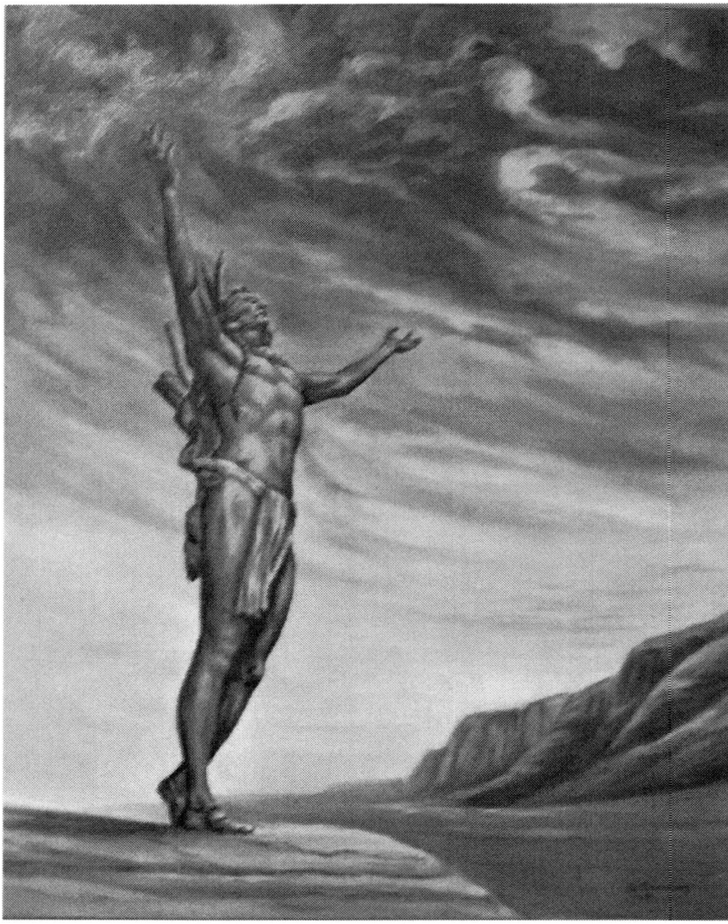

Chapter 8

Whenever we study some of the greatest creators in history, whether they were painters, sculptors, writers, scientists, or inventors and others, we will learn that spending time in solitude was how they were able to make their great contributions to humanity at large. Can we imagine Leonardo de Vinci creating any of his great works of art, such as the MONA LISA, in the midst of other people, or in a noisy setting? I think not. And so it has been for almost all great creators.

Some people may continue to associate solitude with loneliness, but the huge difference is this: Loneliness is marked by a sense of isolation, whereas, solitude, on the other hand, is a state of being alone without being lonely, and it can lead to self-awareness.

In this fast and spinning world that we are living in today, we humans need a variety of ways to deal with all the pressures and schedules in life, and along with that, we need to maintain some semblance of harmony and balance, sensing that we are moving along in the right direction. And if we don't 'get our house in order,' we begin overreacting to the smallest of annoyances, and feeling like we can never catch up; always feeling that 'our ship has left us at the dock.' And let there be no doubt, whenever that situation happens in our life, the best way to counteract it is to seek and enjoy solitude in our life. And perhaps that is where the distinction between solitude and loneliness comes into play. It's important to realize that there's a world of difference between loneliness and solitude, even though the two terms are often used interchangeably. Looking at them from the outside, the two terms may look alike because both are characterized by solitariness, but all resemblance ends at the surface.

Feeling and being lonely is a negative state, and it's marked by a sense of isolation, whereby, we may feel that something is missing, but we can still be with a group of people and continue to feel lonely, which may be the most bitter form of loneliness. One of my strongest memories of feeling lonely was in a church setting, while living in Tennessee. I felt completely alone and alien, as I did not identify with where the preacher and congregation were at in their beliefs and lives. In that setting I heard a lot about sin, the devil and hell, but not enough about peace, our Spirit and love for one and all.

But speaking of solitude, that is a state of being alone without being lonely, because it is a positive and constructive state of engagement with oneself, and...it is a desirable state of being alone where you provide yourself sufficient and wonderful company. To many an ear, that may sound 'crazy,' but being in solitude can be a time used for reflection, growth, or inner searching and enjoyment of some kind. Solitude suggests peacefulness stemming from a state of inner richness. It's a means of enjoying the quiet and whatever it brings that is satisfying, and from which we draw sustenance. Solitude is refreshing, and it is something that we cultivate, because it may not come easy for many people that have conditioned themselves to distractions, noise and chaos. In solitude we have an opportunity to renew ourselves, and it can replenish us, if we only give it a chance. Solitude is something we choose, and loneliness is often imposed on us by others.

It is very important to realize that we all need periods of solitude in our lives, if we are to maintain a sense of harmony and balance with all that we think and do. Solitude gives us time to explore and know ourselves, and especially our "Higher Selves." It also gives us a chance to regain perspective, and it renews us for the challenges of life that can oftentimes be legion. It allows us to get back into the position of driving our own lives, rather than having them run by constant schedules and demands on us from without. In essence, solitude restores our body and mind, whereas... loneliness depletes them! Another great attribute of solitude, it helps us in many ways to be able to share more quality time with other people, when we are together, and offer them insights into things they may be completely unaware of.

Although, in today's society many of us are living alone, but most people are living with other people, and involved with groups of other people, and for some of them, they may be afraid of spending time alone in solitude, and it would be unfamiliar territory in their busy lives, but for those of us who have experienced both, and now living alone, we have found that time in solitude has allowed us to do and create things in a way that could never have been accomplished by being in a group of people, or surrounded by noise, distractions and interruptions.

****

Recently, while watching the morning news on TV, it was so depressing, I chose to turn the news off and go on YouTube to find something peaceful to watch of nature while having my breakfast. And to my great surprise, at the top of the list of films to watch on YouTube was our

Indigenous documentary film called: TRADITIONAL INDIGENOUS WAYS OF BEING. It featured my good Indigenous friends, Apache-Geronimo Vela, Washoe-Dr. Lisa Grayshield and the phenomenal and amazing music by Apaches-Yolanda Martinez and Randy Granger. Although I had watched our film a number of times, since "Spirit" had placed it there for me to watch again on YouTube, I did. And it was 'just what the doctor ordered' for my morning peace of mind. Besides the wonderful commentary in the film by Geronimo Vela and Dr. Lisa Grayshield, and others, I had filmed it in New Mexico, Colorado, Arizona, Utah and Wyoming, and I quickly realized, as I watched the film again, that those spectacular nature scenes of our Sacred Earth Mother never gets tiring or boring to watch. I had filmed all of the documentary's background footage (B-roll) in the five western states while being alone in solitude with nature, and it was so refreshing and healing for my spirit-mind-body to be immersed in nature again by watching our documentary on YouTube. So yes, I thanked our Creator and Spirit Guides of Love and Light for taking me back to the peace and serenity of nature while having breakfast.

It never ceases to amaze me how aware Spirits are of our every move and thought, and when our "channels" are open and ready for them to come in, if we are in solitude and receptive, a wonderful experience, such as I have just mentioned, can take place in our lives.

****

A typical scenario we may wish to consider is of a housewife with a husband and three or four children. While they are all in the house together, the wife and mother may stay quite busy looking after them and their needs, but during the time the husband is away at work and the children are in school, and the wife is a gifted painter, writer, or loves to sew and create things with her hands, there is little doubt that she will treasure her alone time in solitude.

Compared to most men, women have typically, always been multi-taskers, but when they have been given a gift by the Creator to create something that does not involve the family members, she will be driven to find that sacred and special time alone in solitude to fulfill her "Sacred Contract." And some may find fault with that statement, but for just a moment, let's look at the overall health situation of people in the USA today. It has been noted that 66% of our adult population are on prescription drugs. To rid ourselves of "dis-ease," it is very important to be "at-ease," and one of the fastest and best ways to get at ease is being in solitude, where there are no distraction, confusion, noise, etc..

Another important healing method for many of us is to maintain balance and harmony in our lives, and again, spending time alone in solitude is a very effective way to do that. "Be strong enough to stand alone and be yourself enough to stand apart, but be wise enough to stand together when the time comes." So it has been said.

****

IN CONCLUSION: In the present moment that I am writing this, it is 23 October, 2023, and the news media is bombarding us with the war in Israel and Hamas, along with the continual war in Ukraine and Russia. All war is senseless killing of our fellow human beings, from a Spiritual perspective, and for what? I am a firm believer that this physical dimension that we are presently in is an illusion; compared to the higher dimensional realms of Spirit, which, first and foremost, we all are. Yes! I truly believe that we are a Spiritual being on this planet, merely having a 'necessary' physical experience, whereby we are here to experience life and learn things in this primitive dimension of existence, before we return to the Spiritual realm, from whence we came and belong. And for many people, that concept may be difficult to grasp and 'digest,' but it's all about transformation. Perhaps the best example of understanding transformation is 'water.' We all know that liquid water takes on different forms, such as snow, fog, ice, et cetera. And so...it isn't very difficult to understand, if we truly believe that we are first and foremost, a Spiritual being, merely having a physical experience, when the physical body dies and no longer exists, the spirit has left it and moved on into a higher and more real dimension of existence from where it first came and entered into the newborn child at physical birth.

For anyone that may be having a problem understanding the previous statement, my best recommendation would be for that person to make it a priority to find the time to get alone by their self and spend quality time in solitude. And while in solitude it is imperative to detach from the 'whirling and spinning mind-thoughts,' and practice the theory of detachment, detaching from all distracting events and noises, people, places and things that are not relevant on our life-journey, whereby the 'still small voice' can be heard, and the messages we may receive from that 'still small voice' can definitely be wonderful and life-changing, if…we are ready to receive, and…awaken to our HIGHER SELF-SPIRIT, and be in sync with…the ONE AND ALL THAT IS!

PH: (575) 202-8215
edbreeding44@gmail.com

Extensive travel has greatly influenced Ed's perspective of the world. His travels have taken him across all the USA, Canada, Mexico, Honduras, Costa Rica, Cuba, Australia and much of Europe. He served in the U.S. Air Force in Europe, and briefly the CIA in D.C. His managerial position as superintendent with La-Z-Boy Chair Co. in Michigan and Tennessee has greatly helped him deal with a legion of human situations, and expanded his communication skills. His love for interacting with different cultures, metaphysics and the spiritual realm inspire and motivate him, and are often incorporated into his paintings, documentary films and books.

Besides being an avid photographer, for over 30 years Ed's paintings have received National acclaim in the media, exhibitions and galleries, and his paintings graced covers and centerfolds of publications such as WATERFOWL, WATERFOWLER'S WORLD, and AMERICAN FIELD MAGAZINE. His paintings have been known to have a spiritual dimension to many of them. His letters have been published TEN times in USA TODAY Newspaper. Ed's books include: ABSAROKA AWAKENING, A JUST PEACE, FINDING THE AMERICAN MALE, DEATH BEFORE DYING, MURDER ON THE WIND, TULUM, AWAKENDED AND LIVING THEIR TRUTH -A Two-Spirit Odyssey-, LIFE IS A JOURNEY TO HERE(Autobiography), THE RED ROAD, SPIRITS REBELLION and ENCHANTMENT OF NEW MEXICO – A photographic journey-, Paintings of a Lifetime & THE LAND OF EVERMORE. All of his books are available in paperback and Kindle on Amazon.com.

For the past 15 years, besides continuing to paint for four months out of each year, Ed has been greatly involved in making independent documentary films, such as: (Native American films) THE HUMAN EFFECT, MESSAGES FROM THE ANCESTORS, HOLDERS OF

WISDOM, TRADITIONAL INDIGENOUS WAYS OF BEING , UNSHACKLED - and these two films have recently won over 45 International film awards for Best Documentary and Best Cinematography. These documentaries are consistently being shown across the country via FNX (First Nations Experience) PBS TV.

Ed's previous books:

THE BELT AND BEYOND
ABSAROKA AWAKENING
A JUST PEACE
MURDER ON THE WIND
DEATH BEFORE DYING
AWAKENED AND LIVING THEIR TRUTH
LIFE IS A JOURNEY TO HERE (An Autobiography)
FINDING THE AMERICAN MALE
THE RED ROAD
SPIRITS REBELLION
THE LAND OF EVERMORE
PAINTINGS OF A LIFETIME
TULUM
ENCHANTMENT OF NEW MEXICO (A Photographic Journey)
BEYOND BOUNDARIES
A PLACE BEYOND TIME
IVORY & EBONY

(All books available on Amazon)

Ed's Documentary Films:

Wilderness Backpacking in Montana
Love Heals Homophobia
Prescription For Addiction
Genius Sky
Reign Of The Jaguar
Straight Line Curve
Heart of The Arts
Echoes From The Ancestors
Holders of Wisdom
Shattered Reality
Spirit of Art
Messages From The Ancestors
Unshackled
The Human Effect
Traditional Indigenous Ways of Being
Return of The Traditional Indigenous Way

(Available on YouTube/Amazon)

Made in the USA
Columbia, SC
11 February 2024